The Mystery Of The Grail And The

Secret Tradition Of Britain

Lewis Spence

Kessinger Publishing's Rare Reprints

Thousands of Scarce and Hard-to-Find Books on These and other Subjects!

- Americana
- Ancient Mysteries
- Animals
- Anthropology
- Architecture
- Arts
- Astrology
- Bibliographies
- Biographies & Memoirs
- Body, Mind & Spirit
- Business & Investing
- Children & Young Adult
- Collectibles
- Comparative Religions
- Crafts & Hobbies
- Earth Sciences
- Education
- Ephemera
- Fiction
- Folklore
- Geography
- Health & Diet
- History
- Hobbies & Leisure
- Humor
- Illustrated Books
- Language & Culture
- Law
- Life Sciences

- Literature
- Medicine & Pharmacy
- Metaphysical
- Music
- Mystery & Crime
- Mythology
- Natural History
- Outdoor & Nature
- Philosophy
- Poetry
- Political Science
- Science
- Psychiatry & Psychology
- Reference
- Religion & Spiritualism
- Rhetoric
- Sacred Books
- Science Fiction
- Science & Technology
- Self-Help
- Social Sciences
- Symbolism
- Theatre & Drama
- Theology
- Travel & Explorations
- War & Military
- Women
- Yoga
- *Plus Much More!*

**We kindly invite you to view our catalog list at:
http://www.kessinger.net**

CHAPTER VI

THE MYSTERY OF THE GRAIL

SOME recent writers, among them Miss Jessie L. Weston, who speaks with authority, have given it as their opinion that the legend of the Holy Grail, although of British origin, has certainly been sophisticated by Oriental or alien ideas. That may be so, so far as its later elements are concerned, but in its early form it is demonstrably of British provenance, as I hope to prove in this chapter. I also wish to demonstrate that the legend is in direct association with the secret mystical tradition of our island, of the existence of which I have already afforded considerable proof ; that it has indeed a unity with and was drawn from that venerable body of occult belief which I believe is capable of rescue for the use of British mystics.

As I have shown, the poem of Taliesin on "The Spoils of *Annwn*" described the descent of a body of initiates or mystics into the lowest plane or circle, for the express purpose of recovering therefrom the cauldron of Pwyll, the Lord of *Annwn*. In that poem Pwyll and Pryderi, his son, are associated together by name, and the cauldron is found at a place called Caer Sidi or Caer Pedryvan, "the Four-cornered Castle" in the Isle of the Active Door. Now in Norman Grail romances the Grail is said to be in the keeping of Pelles or Peleur, merely Normanized forms of Pwyll, in the Castle of Carbonek, which is merely Caer Bannauc, the "peaked" or "horned" castle, having reference to the points or corners of Caer Sidi.[1]

The vessel which Arthur and his companions recover from *Annwn* is described in the Taliesin poem as a cauldron, the rim of which is set with pearls. The fire beneath it was kindled by the breath of nine maidens, oracular speech emanated from it, and it would not cook the food of a coward. Compare this with the description of the Grail in the Norman romances, where Pelles and his brother are mentioned. The Grail, when it appears, supplies them at the table with whatever kind of food each desires, but the unworthy were not permitted to remain near it or to approach it without hurt to themselves. Those who worship at the Grail Chapel of Peleur remain young, and to them the passage of time signifies nothing. The Grail, too, heals the sick and wounded. It is thus obvious enough that the Grail was nothing more nor less than the magic cauldron of Pwyll given a later Christian interpretation.

The Grail is said to have been brought to Britain by Joseph of Arimathea, who collected the blood of Christ in the vessel and conveyed it to the West, or gave it to one Bron or Brons to convey thither. Brons, it is clear, is merely Bran the Blessed of Welsh literature. Brons, sailing from Palestine, is said to have floated across on a shirt taken from Joseph's Son. But this is nothing but a later "re-hash" of the voyage of Bran to Ireland, to which he is said to have been wafted. Bran, too, or rather his mystical head, which in his legend takes the place of the Grail, provides in Welsh myth banquet and mirth for eight years to his funeral bearers. Rhŷs,

[1] Some authorities give the derivation as Cor-arbenig, "the sovereign chair".

in speaking of the soundness of the comparison, remarks : '' We have in reality to go further : it is not a case of similarity so much as of identity. The voyage of Bron is but a Christian version of the voyage of Bran, and one cannot be surprised to find one of the romances of the Quest of the Holy Grail stating that the vessel was in the keeping of Bron, represented as dwelling 'in these isles of Ireland'.''

In the *Mabinogion* story of Kulhwch and Olwen, Kulhwch is commanded by the giant Yspydaden to procure for him the *Mwys,* or dish of Gwyddno Garanhir. This trencher or platter was capable of feeding all the world, nine at a time, and it was thought to have disappeared with Merlin along with the other treasures of Britain ''when he entered the Glass House in Bardsey.''

But I wish to make it clear that I am here concerned with the Grail romances only in so far as they reveal evidences of the survival of native British mystical tradition. That the Grail tradition was diverted to Christian purposes and therefore penetrated and sophisticated by Christian and Oriental influence is admitted, but with this side of the inquiry I have logically no concern, even with the theory that the Keltic Church in Wales employed the Grail legend to combat the pretensions of the Roman pontiff to British ecclesiastical hegemony. What I look for is evidence of the survival of the original native occult tradition associated with the Grail in its form of a cauldron of inspiration situated on another plane, to reach which initiation into a mystical or Druidic brotherhood was essential.

We have seen that there is actually traditional continuity between the Taliesin poem of ''The Spoils of *Annwn*'' and the Grail legends, that the one arose out of the other, that the Grail was in the first place the cauldron of inspiration of a Druidic cult before it was thought of as the dish which held the blood of the Redeemer.   In one of the later romances it is described as a salver containing a head, in another as a reliquary, again as a "dish" or cup.   It matters not in what form it may appear in Christian symbolism, as it still indubitably retains therein the eucharistic character of its new forms notwithstanding the clearest evidences of its "pagan" or Druidic origins as the Keltic cauldron of inspiration and plenty, the cauldron of the Dagda, of Keridwen, of Pwyll.   Even its Anglo-Norman name, Graal, a dish made of costly materials used for purposes of festival, is merely a translation of the Keltic word *mowys* or *mias*.

In a striking passage on the folklore antecedents of the Grail, Mr. A. E. Waite writes :[1]

> The antecedents of folklore passed into the literature of the Graal undergoing great transmutations, and so also did certain elements of old Druidism merge into Christianity; Rite and Myth and Doctrine were tinged by Tradition and Doctrine and Rite for things which co-exist tend to dovetail, at least by their outer edges; and there are traces, I think, of a time when the priest who said mass at the altar was not only a Druid at heart, but in his heart saw no reason also for the Druid to be priest any less.   Long after the conversion of the Celt, enigmatical fables and mystical Rites lingered in Gaul and Britain, and if one could say that the Cauldron of Ceridwen was a vessel of pagan doctrine, then in an equal symbolical sense it became a vessel of hotch-potch under the strange ægis of the Celtic Church.   There were masters of mysteries and secret science, whose knowledge, it is claimed, was perpetuated under the shadow of that Church and even within the pale thereof.   The Bardic Sanctuary, by the evidence of some who claimed to speak in its name, opposed no precious concealed mysteries, and perhaps on its own part the Church received into its alembic much that was not of its matter, expecting to convert it therein and turn it out in a new form.   In

[1] *The Hidden Church of the Holy Grail*, pp. 176 ff.

the fourth century there were professors at Bordeaux who had once at least been Druids, and for the doctrines of their later reception the heart of their old experience may have been also an alembic. St. Beuno in his last moments is recorded to have exclaimed: " I see the Trinity and Peter and Paul, and the Druids and the Saints!"—a choir invisible, the recognition of which would, if known, have imperilled his canonisation, supposing that its process had been planned in Rome. At a much later period, even in the twelfth century, we have still the indication of perpetuated mysteries, and there is no doubt that the belief in these was promoted generally by the bards. The twelfth century saw also the beginning of a great revival of literature in Wales. There are certain Iolo manuscripts which are late and of doubtful authenticity, but accepting their evidence under all necessary reserves, they refer the revival in question to Rhys ap Twdur, who assumed the sovereignty of South Wales, bringing with him "the system of the Round Table, as it is with regard to min-strels and bards". And when the time came for the last struggle between the Celtic and Latin Rites for the independence of the British Church, I can well believe that all which remained, under all transformations, of that old mixed wisdom of the West was also fighting for its life. When pseudo-Taliesin prophesied the return of Cadwaladr, who had passed into the unmanifest, like Arthur, and, like Arthur, was destined to return, I believe also that this allegory of rebirth or resurrection, if it referred on one side to the aspirations of the Celtic Church did not less embody on another the desired notion of a second spring for the mysteries which once dwelt in Wales, which even after many centuries were interned rather than dead.

But to the tales themselves. The Welsh Perceval or Peredur gives the first form of the Grail legend. We are not here concerned with the story itself, but only with those details in it which illustrate our thesis of the survival of the British tradition.

The mother of Peredur, we are told, had two brothers, Peles and Peleur, as they are called in the Welsh " Seint Greal." These are merely the Pwyll and Pryderi of the old tradition, as has been said. Peredur destroys a monster known as the Addanc or Avanc of the Lake. This was a mighty beaver,

which in another Welsh tale was said to have been
drawn from the waters of its lake by the god or hero
Hu. Now in an ancient Welsh poem, "Cadair
Ceridwen", or "The Chair of Keridwen",[1] the
goddess mentions this animal as follows :

> I saw a fierce conflict in the vale of Beaver, on the
> day of the Sun, at the hour of dawn, between the birds
> of Wrath and Gwydion. On the day of Jove, they (the
> birds of Wrath) securely went to Mona, to demand a
> sudden shower of the sorcerers; but the goddess of the
> silver wheel,[2] of auspicious mien, the dawn of serenity,
> the greatest restrainer of sadness, in behalf of the Britons,
> speedily throws round his hall the stream of the Rainbow,
> a stream which scares away violence from the earth, and
> causes the bane of its former state, round the circle of
> the world, to subside. The books of the Ruler of the
> Mount record no falsehood. The Chair of the Preserver
> remains here; and till the doom, shall it continue in
> Europe.

Thus the Avanc and Keridwen, goddess of the
cauldron, are associated, and the whole passage
unquestionably relates to a part of the ceremony of
initiation into the rites of Keridwen, goddess of the
cauldron of inspiration, a passage referring to the
strife between sun and storm, order and chaos, and
one which could be equated from the rituals of more
than one secret tradition.

Next the castle visited by Peredur, and which is
obviously the Castle of the Grail and the Fisher King
(for the Welsh version is later and probably borrowed
much of its "machinery" from Norman sources) is
merely the Palace of Caer Sidi or Caer Bannauc, the
royal seat of *Annwn*, the centre of the mysteries of
the Astral Plane, where the cauldron of inspiration
(or Grail) was kept. Here he meets the owner of
the Castle, his uncle (the "Fisher King" of the Grail
versions) who was watching his men fishing in the

[1] *Welsh Archaeology*, p. 66.   [2] Arianrhod.

lake. He tells Peredur, in the true accents of one who has arcane knowledge to conceal, that whatever strange things he may see in the castle, he must not speak of.

The late Mr. Alfred Nutt believed that in the original Keltic tradition the surname of the Fisher King had a significance now lost.[1] Now the brother of this Fisher King is called in the Norman-French Grail romances Goon Desert, Gornumant, and Gonemans, which, as Rhŷs has shown,[2] are merely corruptions of the name of Gwyn, son of Nudd, King of the demons of the Otherworld. Now Gwyn, in Welsh myth, has a brother or companion Gwydno, whose name seems to have meant ''Tall Crane'', or ''Stalking Person'', and he was famous as the owner of a weir in which fish to the value of a hundred pounds were caught on the eve of the First of May each year. Connected with this story was the legend of the finding of the babe Taliesin in this weir, as recorded beforehand, that Taliesin, indeed, who was the son of Keridwen, born to her after she had swallowed Gwion, the watcher of her cauldron, that very Taliesin who was the ''official'' bard of the mysteries of Caer Sidi or *Annwn*, and who boasts that he was present with Arthur when he stole the cauldron of inspiration therefrom, whose ''rebirth'', as Canon MacCulloch acutely observes, ''is connected with his acquiring of inspiration''.[3]

It is thus clear enough that the whole Grail myth is founded in the central idea of the cauldron of inspiration in *Annwn*, the mystical plane, that this is, indeed, the hub from which all the spokes of the wheel radiate. *The Red Book of Hergest,* of which the Welsh ''Peredur'' or ''Perceval'' is a part, is

[1] *Holy Grail,* p. 123. [2] *Arthurian Legend,* pp. 315-16.
[3] op. cit. p. 118.

found in a Welsh manuscript of the end of the thirteenth century, so that at that relatively late date we find the initiation story of the *Annwn* Plane, somewhat garbled, perhaps, but still flourishing, if with a Christian interpretation.

The *Conte del Graal* of Robert de Borron and his continuators, commenced about the third quarter of the twelfth century, is "a composition", says Rhŷs,[1] "which cannot help striking a student of Welsh literature and mythology as one of the oldest in point of time and allusion within the whole cycle of Grail romance." It says of the Rich Fisher : "much knew he of black art, more than an hundred times changed he his semblance".

Now the whole turning-point and key of the *Conte del Graal* is connected with the mystic question which Perceval fails to put to the Fisher King, the "suppressed word", as Mr. Waite calls it. "In the *Conte del Graal*," he writes,[2] "the law and order of the Quest is that Perceval shall ask the meaning of these wonders which he sees in the pageant at the Castle of the Quest." The prime question he should have put to the sick Fisher King was : "Unto whom one serveth of the Graal?" and this query would have released the King from his mystical dumbness and have permitted him to pass on the translation of the Secret Words, the keys of the mystery he conserved, and have dispelled the Enchantment of Britain. Because he did not ask the question Perceval was assailed with reproaches.

If we look a little more closely into the story of the Lame Fisher King and his brother we find plenty of evidence that they are the people of the Underworld well defined in myth. In the first place, the ruler of Hades is frequently lame, and Vulcan,

---

[1] op. cit. p. 117.   [2] op. cit. p. 153.

Weyland Smith and even the mediæval Satan show this deformity. Pwyll, or the Fisher King, is, indeed, the grand black magician of the Underworld, who, still, has the means of fertility, inspiration and regeneration in his mystical cauldron.

The three properties of the cauldron—inexhaustibility, inspiration, and regeneration—may be summed up in one word, fertility; and it is significant that the (Irish) god with whom such a cauldron was associated, Dagda, was a god of fertility. But we have just seen it associated, directly or indirectly, with goddesses—Cerridwen, Branwen, the women from the lake—and perhaps this may point to an earlier cult of goddesses of fertility, later transferred to gods. In this light the cauldron's power of restoring to life is significant, since in early belief life is associated with what is feminine. . . . Again, the slaughter and cooking of animals was usually regarded as a sacred act in primitive life. The animals were cooked in enormous cauldrons, which were found as an invariable part of the furniture of every Celtic house. The quantities of meat which they contained may have suggested inexhaustibility to people to whom the cauldron was already a symbol of fertility. Thus the symbolic cauldron of a fertility cult was merged with the cauldron used in the religious slaughter and cooking of animal food. The cauldron was also used in ritual. The Cimri slaughtered human victims over a cauldron and filled it with their blood. . . .

Like the food of men, which was regarded as the food of the gods, the cauldron of this world became the marvellous cauldron of the Otherworld, and as it then became necessary to explain the origin of such cauldrons on earth, myths arose, telling how they had been stolen from the divine land by adventurous heroes, Cuchulainn, Arthur, etc. In other instances, the cauldron is replaced by a magic vessel or cup stolen from supernatural beings of the Fionn saga or of *marchen*. Here, too, it may be noted that the Graal of Arthurian romance has affinities with the Celtic cauldron. . . . Thus in the Graal there was a fusion of the magic cauldron of Celtic paganism and the Sacred Chalice of Christianity, with the product made mystic and glorious in a most wonderful manner.[1]

[1] MacCulloch, op. cit. pp. 382-3.

In fact the whole myth explains the bringing of the mystical tradition, the Essence of Divine Life, and all that it implied from another plane, just as domestic animals such as the pig, the dog, and the deer were also brought from that plane, or as fire was thought of as having been brought from heaven by Prometheus, or cattle from ''Fairyland''. Long afterwards, as folk-tale assures us, the notion lingered that all good gifts emanated from the Underworld, and many are the stories told of men and women who penetrated the fairy-hill to gain either hidden lore or magical objects, as we shall see when we come to consider the subject in its folklore aspect. In numerous instances these had first to lose their senses, to become unconscious or fall asleep before admittance to the fairy realm. The Grail legends are merely Christianized versions of this theme, glorified and sanctified to fit them to the more exalted aim. They enshrine the remains of an ancient British code of initiation deflected to the uses of Christianity.

We have seen that in some versions of the Grail legend Peredur or Perceval is told by the Fisher King that he must *not* ask the reason of anything he beholds, whereas in the others he is blamed for refraining from putting the question. The second is manifestly a perversion of the first, obviously designed for later religious reasons. To ask the reason of any mystery in the Land of Enchantment or to put questions to any enchanted person is speedily to meet with disaster. It is a relic of an ancient system of taboos. Peredur must not interrogate the King of *Annwn* on matters relating to the mysteries of the Underworld, simply because the replies to these would instantly have placed that ruler's occult power in the hands of another.

The Grail as a cauldron may for a moment attract our attention. The cauldron is a symbol of the magical brew, and as such has its later counterpart in the witches' cauldron. Now from one point of view the cauldron is obviously, besides being the symbol of inspiration, plenty, and fertility, the symbol of *Annwn* itself, the region or plane in which the lower life which was sooner or later to overflow into *Abred*, the earth-plane, seethed and bubbled. It is the symbol of life, psychical as well as physical, germinating and evolving. Moreover, the myth of Arthur's journey to *Annwn* is an allegory of the ascent from *Annwn*, through initiation, into *Abred*. The "life" which seethes in the cauldron of Pwyll is removed by the initiates to a higher plane. It is obviously a myth of the evolution of life and spirit from a lower to a more exalted sphere. It follows that there was probably a similar story, now lost, of the evolution of soul-life from *Abred* to *Gwynvyd*, the sphere of immortal beings, the whole composing an allegory of the soul's journey.

CHAPTER VII

THE SECRET TRADITION IN RITE AND LEGEND

THE ancient secret tradition of Britain survives in a fragmentary manner in numerous legends, local customs and festivals, in curious rites connected with such localities as holy wells and in other manifestations. It is, of course, questionable how far some of these are associated with the ancient occult tradition of the island, and many of them may be merely survivals of the popular beliefs which constituted its baser side, bearing, indeed, the same relationship to the philosophical part of it, the official cult, so to speak, as do the rites of the Sudra caste of India to Brahminism. For what was preserved by popular favour alone could scarely have been of much mystical value in the higher sense, or have enjoyed much official countenance. At the same time, popular rites and festivals may have conserved certain ideas capable of throwing light on the Secret Tradition, especially in so far as they may be of Iberian origin. With those which have no bearing on the Secret Tradition we are, of course, not concerned.

In the first place, it is notable that the idea of *Annwn*, the mystic plane to which Arthur and his companions were thought to have penetrated, still survives as a part of modern Welsh folklore. The late Sir John Rhŷs, in his *Celtic Folklore*, provides many traditions of *Annwn*, how the "Plant Annwn", or denizens of that realm, were wont to penetrate to this upper world, hunting the souls of doomed men who had died without baptism or penance with their ban-hounds. Indeed, they came into such close contact with the sons of men that the latter were actually able to capture one of their milk-white kine !

Strangely enough we do not find any reminiscences in modern Keltic folklore of the other planes in the mystic circle, but that merely implies that the circle of *Annwn* was believed to lie much nearer that of *Abred*, the dwelling-place of man, than the others, and that therefore communication with it was much more common.

Now there is some evidence that Arthur, in his mythological aspect, superseded, or was a "surrogate" of a certain Hu Gadarn, who, we will remember, was responsible for dragging the Avanc or monster of the lake from his watery abyss by means of large horned oxen. It seems, indeed, that at one time a complete saga must have existed of the Harrying of Hell by this Hu, of which the capture of the Avanc and the raid for the Cauldron were subsidiary parts ; that the manner in which the secrets of the mystical plane of *Annwn* had been recovered by the brotherhood of an occult priesthood had been digested into writing or into these mnemonic poems of which the British Druids were wont to make use. In his *Celtic Folklore* Sir John Rhŷs makes it plain that modern Welsh peasants believe Arthur to have been the hero of the Avanc exploit rather than Hu the mighty. It would seem, therefore, that Arthur has taken over many of Hu's attributes and adventures.

But that the rites of Hu Gadarn or Arthur—for the two are, as we shall see, one and the same— survived until the middle of the sixteenth century at least is plain from several passages in English and Welsh literature. One of the objects of pilgrimage in the Principality prior to the Reformation was the image of Darvell Gadarn in the Diocese of St. Asaph.   In a letter from Ellis Price to Cromwell, Secretary to Henry VIII., dated April 6th, 1538, the image is described as follows :

> There ys an Image of Darvellgadarn within the said diocese, in whome the people have so great confidence, hope, and truste, that they cumme dayly a pillgramage unto hym, somme with kyne, other with oxen or horsis, and the reste withe money ; in so much that there was fyve or syxe hundrethe pilgrimes to a mans estimacion, that offered to the said image the fifte daie of this presente monethe of Aprill.   The innocente people hath ben sore aluryd and entised to worship the saide image, in so much that there is a commyn sayinge as yet amongst them that who so ever will offer anie thinge to the saide Image of Darvellgadern, he hathe power to fatche hym or them that so offers oute of Hell when they be dampned.

Now this idol was taken to Smithfield in the same year and burned.   It is obvious, of course, that Darvell Gadarn and Hu Gadarn are one and the same.   Besides, it was peculiarly the province of Hu Gadarn to draw souls out of *Annwn*, or "Hell". He was the supreme deity, who by the strength of his emanations (his solar oxen) drew the Avanc or beaver (the sun) out of the lake, an allegory of his ability to rescue life from the darkness of the abyss.

Now all this points to the existence and functioning of the ancient British Tradition in the sixteenth century at least, for the worship of a deity like Darvell Gadarn could not have existed in Wales unless it were associated with a mystic brotherhood or priesthood, without whom it would have had no sanction or status, no binding force.   And this is rather borne out by the fact that when the idol was taken to Smithfield there was taken with it a "friar" *who bore the same name as itself*, and who was also committed to the flames.   Had he been a friar in Holy

Orders such a fate would certainly not have been meted out to him, nor could he have borne such a name, and it therefore appears as if he must have been not only the living representative of the god, but the conservator of his mysteries and the ancient British Secret Tradition, visited by hundreds of pilgrims, who worshipped the idol as a quite familiar deity.[1]

It is also to be noticed that oxen were offered up to this image. This not only makes it plain that it represented the Hu Gadarn of Welsh myth, but that it was identified with the sacred solar ox or bull symbolic of that deity, and which we have seen was referred to in more than one of the British mystical poems.

In the superstition concerning changelings, we also find a very distinct trace of a belief in the return of the soul to the dreary region of *Annwn*. The superstition ran that the fairies frequently exchanged their offspring for that of human beings, leaving behind a withered and often half-idiot elf in place of the robust human babe which they had spirited away. As we have already seen, the belief in fairies probably originated from the Cult of the Dead. That is, they were supposed to be the (evil?) dead waiting for re-birth, and that they were also associated with *Annwn* is positive. The changeling was thus a soul from *Annwn*, struggling to get a hold on *Abred*, the earth-plane, whereas the belief that it was possible for the fairies to spirit children away seems to have arisen from the idea that the human soul, if its earth-journey were not satisfactory, might once more lapse into the depths of *Annwn*.

In a word, the superstition about changelings is

[1] The worship of Hu Gadarn in Wales at such a late date as 1538 suffices to quash utterly the arguments of the opponents of the theory that Druidism collapsed in Roman times.

undoubtedly a memory of a cult which believed in the progression or retrogression of souls rather than in their transmigration.   For after all, there is very little evidence that transmigration in its usually accepted form was believed in by our forefathers, whereas there is abundant proof that a great scheme of psychic evolution underlay their theology.   A ceremony which has also obvious relationships to the belief in the plane of *Annwn*, and which, indeed, displays the remains of mystic rites associated with the ancient brotherhood who presided over its ritual, is that of Hallow-e'en.

In his account of the Bards, Owen tells us that in North Wales the first day of November was attended by many ceremonies, such as lighting a large fire and running through it, "running away to escape from the black short-tailed sow", and so forth. He says :

> " Amongst the first aberrations may be traced that of the knowledge of the great Huon or the Supreme Being, which was obscured by the hieroglyphics or emblems of his different attributes, so that the grovelling minds of the multitude often sought not beyond those representations for the objects of worship and adoration.   This opened an inlet for numerous errors more minute; and many superstitions became attached to their periodical solemnities and more particularly to their rejoicing fires and the appearance of vegetation in spring and of the completion of harvest in autumn."

Huon is, of course, the same as Hu Gadarn, so that here once more we find him associated with a rite of the Underworld, for the Hallow-e'en fire was nothing more or less than a symbol of that of *Annwn*, as is easily proved by the reference to the "black short-tailed sow".   The reader will remember that the pig was one of the "Spoils of *Annwn*", given to the earth by Pwyll.   The minister of Kirkmichael in Perthshire, writing in the Statistical

Account, says : " Formerly the Hallow Even Fire, a relic of Druidism, was kindled in Buchan, various magic ceremonies were then celebrated to counteract the influences of witches and demons. . . . Societies were formed, either by pique or humour, to scatter certain fires, and the attack and defence were often conducted with art and fury." It is surely clear enough that this rite, totally unlike the more innocent amusements associated with Hallowe'en in more modern times, was the memorial of a very ancient myth interpreted by dramatic action, descriptive of the attack on the fiery underworld plane by a society or brotherhood of mystics. Dramas of the kind were invariably associated with the Mysteries of the ancient world, in Greece and Egypt especially. And that these celebrations were popularly believed to have descended from the Druids is not only stated by the minister of Kirkmichael, but by the minister of Callander, who in the same Account states that : "The people received the consecrated fire from the Druid priests next morning, the virtues of which were supposed to continue for a year."

It is by no means a simple task to trace the eroded outline of the mystical tradition of Britain in folk-belief and legend, and in many instances the professional exponents of Folklore have made the task all the more difficult by their insistence in regarding all ancient beliefs as having a bearing on vegetation or other rites, neglecting altogether the deeper significance which lies beneath these tales. In order to prove that a recognized caste of celebrants did actually exist within living memory, I will now turn to various evidences of their presence, in Wales at least. In Lewis's *Topographical Dictionary of Wales* we read that the Well of Fynnon Elian "Even in the present age is frequently visited by the superstitious . . . the ceremonies performed by the applicant standing upon a certain spot near the well while the owner of it reads a few passages of the sacred Scriptures, and then taking a small quantity of water gives it to the former to drink, throwing the residue over his head, which is repeated three times." Foulkes, in his *Enwogion Cymru*, published in 1870, says that the last person to have charge of the Well was a certain John Evans. Before him a woman had officiated there and many amusing tales of her shrewdness were recounted. Says Rhŷs in his *Celtic Folklore*:

> A series of articles on the Well appeared in 1861 and were afterwards published, I am told, as a shilling book which I have not seen, and they dealt with the superstition, with the history of John Evans, and with his confessions and *conversions*.[1]   I have searched in vain for any accounts in Welsh of the ritual followed at the Well. When Mrs. Silvan Evans visited the place the person in charge of the Well was a woman, and Peter Roberts in his *Cambrian Popular Antiquities*, published in London in 1815, alludes to her or a predecessor of hers in the following terms: " Near the well resided some worthless and infamous wretch who officiated as priestess. . . ." There is, I think, very little doubt that the owner or guardian of the Well was, so to say, the representative of an ancient priesthood of the Well. That priesthood dated its origin probably many centuries before a Christian church was built near the Well, and coming down to later times, we have unfortunately no sufficient data to show how the right to such priesthood was acquired, whether by inheritance or otherwise; but we know that a woman might have charge of St. Elian's Well.

Sir John also left behind him data regarding a similar site in Pembrokeshire, the Church of St. Teilo. The building, he tells us, is in ruins, but the church-yard is still used and contains two of the most ancient post-Roman inscriptions in the Principality. This well was thought to be good for the whooping-cough,

---

[1] Italics mine.—L.S.

and when Sir John made inquiries as to whether any rite or ceremony must be performed in order to derive benefit from the water, he was told that the water must be lifted out of the well and given to the patient to drink by somebody *born in the adjoining house, preferably by the heir*. The water, it appears, was drawn from the well in a skull which was said to be the skull of St. Teilo, and, indeed, he was shown the skull. Sir John learned later that this well is known as the *Oxen's Well*, and that the family owning and occupying the adjoining farmhouse *had been there for centuries*. Their name was Melchior, by no means a common one in the Principality, and having a sound sufficiently priestly, in all conscience. There was also current a legend relating to the manner in which the skull came to be used as a drinking vessel. "In this particular instance," says Sir John Rh ̂ys, " we have a succession which seems to point unmistakeably to an ancient priesthood of a sacred spring."

Now mark that this well was known as the "Oxen's Well", that is, it was associated in some manner with the cult of Hu Gadarn, the mystic deity of the Brythonic race who with his sacred oxen was supposed to have overcome the powers of evil. Here we have a case, as Rh ̂ys, a very sound authority, was convinced, *of the survival of a hereditary priesthood in Wales from pre-Christian times until the beginning of the twentieth century!* We seem to have clear evidence not only that such a cult actually existed, but that it was in some way associated with the mystic ox and thus with the occult brotherhood who were led by Arthur into the gloomy abyss of *Annwn*.

Elsewhere on British soil there are evidences of the existence of persons who appear to have been inculcated into a mysterious and magical society whose writings they actually preserved. A woman attainted by the Presbytery of Perth for sorcery in 1626 stated that she had a book containing magical knowledge which was her "Goodsire's, her Grandsire's, and was a thousand years old." Her son, Adam Bell, read it to her. Again there are many proofs, as we shall see when we come to deal with the cult of witchcraft, of persons being initiated into the ritual of that cult either by their relatives or by friends.

It will be necessary to say a word here regarding Arthur's glass-ship, alluded to in the legend of the descent into *Annwn*. This vessel has been construed by various authorities as a diving-bell, and so forth, and has been equated with the boat of glass in Irish myth in which Condla the Red was spirited away to the Land of the Everliving by a fairy princess. But I think it is obvious that the vessel has more a spiritual than a material significance, that, indeed, it more nearly resembles the ship of the Egyptian Osiris, which was supposed to navigate the dark waters of Amenti, the Egyptian Underworld. The two myths are, indeed, one, and obviously emanate from a common source. This craft is, indeed, the ship of souls, just as is the barque of Osiris, and in this connection we may recall the myth cited by the late Greek writer Procopius, quoted at the commencement of this volume, in which he describes the passage of the dead souls by ship to the shores of Britain. This proves that a very ancient myth actually existed relative to the bearing of the souls of the departed into the land of darkness by means of a magical vessel. This magical vessel was, indeed, the vehicle by which the astral shape was transported into its appropriate plane, and, in the case of Arthur and his comrades, it was obviously able to transport also the astral shapes of the living to an extra-terrestrial sphere. What was the nature of this vessel?

That this ship had a solar significance we may be pretty certain. The similar Egyptian barque which plumbed the depths of Amenti was certainly of solar origin, and its symbolical significance seems to be that of light invading darkness, the ship of the Sun god penetrating the gloom of the world of Death or non-being.

Perhaps the derivation of Caer Sidi, a part of *Annwn*, is, as Rhŷs thought, Caer Shee, "City of the Fairies". It is notable that four organs play around its fire. This instrument has a long association with mysteries, from those of Byzantium to the present day, as in Masonry.

Searching through the detritus of Folklore for evidences of the Secret Tradition, we have now to consider what precisely were its associations, if any, with the cult known as witchcraft. What exactly was witchcraft, and was it intimately associated with the ancient Secret Tradition of Britain? We are now aware that witchcraft was by no means a thing of hallucination, that it did not originate in the imaginations of disgruntled old women. Research has made it abundantly clear that, as known in the sixteenth and seventeenth centuries, it was the last remaining fragment of a very ancient cult, which probably had its origin in prehistoric times. I believe it to have had its beginnings in a caste of women associated with horse-breeding or cattle-raising, or both, as the entire folklore of the cult has reminiscences of association with the horse and with domestic cattle. Some such caste, I think, as that of the Amazons of classical lore may possibly have been the prototype of the witch cult. The tendency of the witch to bespell cattle, her obvious power over flocks and herds, and her traditional aspect as a horse-using sorceress has led me to believe that somewhere in North-West Africa a female religion arose out of the usages of such a body of women as I describe, which later lost its significance with respect to pastoral affairs, and became purely and simply magical and occult. That it was thus of "Iberian" origin is also highly probable, and thus it was bound to have been connected with that general aboriginal body of faith and superstition on which Druidism was founded, that, indeed, it represented the lower *cultus* in Britain and elsewhere, an aboriginal faith.

Although we do not hear a great deal about it in British history, there is no doubt that witchcraft, as a more or less secret cult, persisted in Britain throughout the ages, but I do not believe it to have been part of Druidism or of the Secret Tradition. Rather was it a debased remnant of that still older Iberian magic which to some extent Druidism embraced, but which it also superseded and perhaps tried to weed out. As Sir James Frazer has shown in his *Golden Bough*, the Druids seem to have burned animals whom they believed to be witches in disguise, and *a fortiori*, it seems probable that they also burned sorcerers, male or female, on occasion. The Druidic priestesses of whom we read, those for example of the Island of Sena, or of Anglesey, although perhaps acting as a separate female caste, do not appear to have been of the character of witches. There is, however, one connection between the nine muse-like maidens who kept the Cauldron of Keridwen warm, and who have been identified with the priestesses of Sena, and the cult of more modern witchcraft, and that is the Cauldron itself.

But was the witch's cauldron of tradition the same

as that of Keridwen? The Cauldron of Keridwen was obviously a vessel of inspiration, whereas the cauldron of the witches was a vessel for the brewing of poisonous concoctions. We will remember, however, that the contents of Keridwen's Cauldron were of a poisonous nature with the exception of the first three drops which sprang from it, and this would seem to link it with the magical vessel of the witches. I do not believe, however, that this cauldron was originally part and parcel of the witch's magical apparatus. I rather incline to think, as the evidence tends to show, that it had been adopted by the members of the witch-cult from that which conserved the Secret Tradition.

For these and other reasons I do not think that the witch-cult had any connection, official or otherwise, with that of Druidism or the Secret Tradition. I rather believe, as I have already said, that it arose out of the ancient aboriginal or Iberian body of gross superstition once existing in Britain, Gaul and Spain. But it seems to me extremely probable that it borrowed much from the cult of the Secret Tradition, especially as regards some of its ritual practices, which it would debase and turn to evil uses.

Many of the magical acts of the witches are identical with those which are alluded to as having been practised by the Druids, such as levitation, the raising of storms, the use of herbs, transformation into animal shapes and so forth, and it may be that the lower castes of official Druidism actually employed stratagems of the kind which they had borrowed from the practitioners of the aboriginal religion for the purpose of overawing the people, just as the earliest Christian disciples in Britain and elsewhere seem to have used a certain amount of low-caste black magic for a similar purpose.

We now come to evidence which makes it plain that a strong leaven of the old Druidic cult, the vehicle of the Secret Tradition, survived until what may be called comparatively recent times in Scotland. As late as 1649 to 1678, according to the records of the Presbytery of Dingwall, bulls were sacrificed in the parish of Gairloch in Ross-shire and oblations of milk poured on the hills.

The Rev. James Rust, minister of Slains, in his *Druidism Exhumed,* published in 1871, provides the following valuable evidence of the survival of Druidic belief in eighteenth century Scotland.[1]

> As there was in the seventeenth century a number of superstitions prevalent in Scotland, as well as in England, which had come into being in Popish times, as well as a number which had had an existence before Popish times, belonging to the earlier system of religion, the Druidical, and which had been tolerated, connived at, or at least not extirpated, the General Assembly of the Church of Scotland resolved to take action against them. As the most of these superstitions, they said, proceeded from ignorance, they resolved that the most strenuous efforts should be made throughout Scotland for bringing education to the doors of all, even of the poorest, by the erection and extension of Parochial Schools, and by urging that Bibles should be possessed in every family, and the inmates taught to read them. But besides this, they appointed a Commission. The General Assembly of 1649 approving of a recommendation of the Assembly 1647, appointed a large Commission of their own number. Along with the Ministers appointed, there were Sir Archibald Johnston of Warristoun, "Clerk Register"; Mr. Thomas Nicholson, "His Majesty's Advocate"; Mr. Alexander Pierson, one of the ordinary "Lords of Session", Sir Lewis Stewart, Mr. Alexander Colvill, and Mr. James Robertson, "Justice Deputes"; Messrs. Rodger Mowet, John Gilmoir, and John Nisbet, "Lawyers"; with Doctors Sibbald, Cunninghame, and Purves, "Physicians". And they did "ordain the said brethren to make report of the result of their consultations and conferences from time to time, as they make any considerable progress, to the Commission for public affairs. And the said Commission

[1] pp. 38 ff.

shall make report to the next General Assembly''. Among other matters, to which they directed their attention, were the Druidical customs observed at the fires of Beltane, Midsummer, Halloweven, and Yuil. All these customs and fires were ordered to be abolished. They succeeded outwardly among the old, although the youth of the country still enjoy in many places some of these same customs and fires, although they have forgotten the object of their institution, and of course the superstition itself. They directed their attention to the Remains of Druidical Superstition and Sorcery practised at the old places of worship, dedicated not only to the greater, but to the lesser gods, the familiar spirits, the household divinities, or demigods of the ancients, who, as was supposed, could be consulted, and could grant charming powers to their votaries, at those pieces of ground which the Druids had consecrated to them, and which had continued for thousands of years untilled. These were ordered to be cultivated under severe church censures and civil penalties, church and state then acting hand in hand in the matter. As one of the results of this Commission, we find some most important minutes in the Kirk Session Register Book of Slains, stating that inquisition was made by the minister and Elders of Slains,—as must have been done by other Ministers and Sessions,—into old Druidical superstitious practices and places within the parish. And from that inquisition, we learn that within Slains there were different pieces of land dedicated to the demi-gods of the Druids, those imps who became the little elfin tricky semidemons of the Christians; and that these places were called after those fancied creatures by words both of Lowland Scots and Highland Gaelic, as the *Guidmanes fauld*, and *Garlet*, or *Garleachd*, connected with Garlaoch, An Elf.

From entries in the Kirk Session Register Book of the Parish of Slains we find that several persons were "delaytit" or summoned before it for practising pagan rites in connection with hallow fires and refusing to till the ancient Druidical fields.

Here then we have the General Assembly of the Church of Scotland only 280 years ago, or but four "lifetimes" since, fully persuaded that Druidism was being practised all over Scotland, and taking steps to put it down. How those steps were received by

L

their congregations is probably well illustrated by Mr. John Buchan's most interesting novel *Witch Wood.*

In writing further of the antiquities of his parish, Mr. Rust deals with the belief that the spirits of the Keltic past were wont to manifest themselves on occasion to the people in old times, who were not infrequently decoyed into the recesses of the earth. There was at least three places within the Parish of Slains dedicated to the "Good People", and these remained uncultivated in the midst of cultivated ground until the beginning of the nineteenth century. " It continued also to be employed for generations for magical superstitious purposes, after the other Elfin places had been destroyed, desecrated, or cultivated by authority. I knew the woman, Mary Findlay, who died a few years ago at a great age, who was the last person laid down in infancy at the Cairn, because she was supposed to be an Elfin Changeling."

But let us examine what he says regarding the Lykar Cairn :

Lykar Cairn lay eight hundred yards N.N.E. of the Parish Church in the south angle formed by the Castle Road, where it diverges from the Turn-the-neuk Road, in a small valley surrounded by natural eminences or knolls, the most striking of which, and to the base of which it was nearest, is *Maidsemaaighe*, which means "The knoll of the very great caldron". It comes from *Maidse*, fem. "A knoll, lump, or hillock": and *ma*, a comparative with a superlative meaning, of *mor*, *great*, and *aighe*, a genitive of *aghann*, fem. a *caldron*. This will turn out, as we shall find, to have the same meaning as Bennachie, and it will contribute to make a most interesting disclosure of the Druidical religious system. We shall therefore reserve the further consideration of this till we come to consider under a distinct branch, and in a subsequent part, the Utensil or Structure called "The Caldron", so much celebrated in Welsh Mythology, but of which no notice has been taken in Scotland, although we might upon the smallest reflection have anticipated that what prevailed, or existed in the one place, did so originally in the other.

So the Cauldron of Keridwen was associated with the survival of Druidic belief in Scotland so lately as the close of the seventeenth century! Mr. Rust points out that this name "the Cauldron" is connected with numerous localities in Scotland, at Aberdeen (Kettle-hill or Cadhal, a cauldron), where, according to local tradition, the cauldron "was made by the Picts", and was used by large crowds "for religious purposes". Place-names, too, in which enter the word Aden, Eden or Edin, as in Edinburgh, were, thought Rust, connected with the cult of the cauldron, from the Gaelic Aidheann, "a cauldron, kettle, or goblet".

"The drinking of the water of this cauldron," says Mr. Rust, "was one of the rites of the Novitiate's Initiation into the Druidical mysteries and craft, after twenty years of hard study. It was the previous hard study, and not the caldron decoction, which made him so great an adept in the Druidical art and science, and opened up futurity to his view. The Novitiate promised to the admitting Hierophant and his three accompanying Druids, during the dark hours of night, that he would be faithful to the Druidical caste. And the most fearful oaths were undertaken by him, and as dreadful orgies gone through by him."

"In Bennachie, a Druidical locality," says Rust, "is the 'Maiden Casay', or Mha-adhann-casach, 'The Great Cauldron Ascent', and 'The Maiden Stene', or Mha-adhann-lia, 'The Very Great Cauldron Stone', the Cauldron on which has been removed, probably when the modern road was formed." But upon the stone itself is incised a figure which Rust believed to be a representation of the Cauldron itself. "The Structure," he says, "according to the figure, allowed the flames to play below and around the Caldron, which was always seething with its mysterious and wonder-working contents. It is," says Rust, "the holy Caldron, the Caldron of knowledge and initiation, for it has the Z figure passing through it. This Z figure has been erroneously styled sometimes the Broken Spear, and sometimes the Broken Sceptre, and because neither of these was satisfactory it has been sometimes called by others just the Z figure, because it resembles that letter of the alphabet; and they could not think of anything else upon which they could agree. But that Figure is just the zigzag lightning of Heaven, drawn down by the Druids, who pretended to be possessed of this divine power. By this, they alleged, they produced the real celestial fire, which they sold to their votaries for domestic purposes at so dear a rate, but, according to their accounts and belief, so worthy of the price. This belief in the Heaven-produced fire was firm, deep, and universal."

That pagan rites in Scotland were regarded as "common usage" is rendered clear enough from a passage in the *Chronicle of Lanercost* (Bk. II, ch. viii), from which it appears that John, the parish priest of Inverkeithing, in Fife, was cited before his bishop in 1282 for having celebrated Easter Week "according to the rites of Priapus" by collecting the maidens of the town and making them dance round the figure of the phallic deity, singing the while. He pleaded the "common usage of the country" and was allowed to retain his benefice. This is precisely what was done, so far as the date was concerned, by the priest of Darvel Gadarn in Wales, who celebrated his highest rites on April 5th, Easter Day. There is no doubt that the stern battle of the early Keltic Church for a separate Easter arose out of especial veneration for a Keltic seasonal festival of great antiquity.

It cannot but be interesting to us to examine briefly such of the Druidic rites whose details are known in order to discover how much light these may cast upon the Secret Tradition. The rite which perhaps has been described more frequently than any other was that of the ceremonial gathering of the mistletoe. From the accounts of Pliny and Maximus of Tyre we know that the oak tree was sacred to the Kelts, and it therefore follows that the gathering of the mistletoe was definitely associated with the fundamentals of their faith. The Druidical groves were composed of oak trees, and the sacred ceremonies of the Druids were invariably graced by the presence of oak branches. In short, the oak tree was in itself a deity.

The mistletoe is not frequently found on the oak, it is more apt to twine parasitically on the poplar and the willow. Its precise significance, I believe, has been altogether missed by the majority of those writers who have dealt with this aspect of it. It has been thought to be a sign of the especial favour of the god, the symbol of immortality, of lightning, and so forth! But I believe it to be the symbol of the essence of life, regarded by the ancients indeed as the protoplasmic material of existence.

It was culled on the sixth day of the moon. Extraordinary preparations for feast and sacrifice were made beneath the tree which bore it, says Pliny, and two white bulls whose horns had never been bound were conveyed thither. A white-clad Druid climbed the tree and cut the mistletoe with a golden sickle.

As it fell it was caught in a white cloth. The bulls were then sacrificed and prayers offered up to the god. Among the Kelts the mistletoe was known as an "all-heal", and the liquor brewed from it was supposed to make barren animals fruitful, a fact which buttresses my contention that it was regarded as the protoplasm of life. Canon MacCulloch wisely sees in Pliny's account the description of a rite which "was an attenuated survival of something which had once been important, but it is more likely that Pliny gives only a few picturesque details, and passes by the rationale of the ritual. He does not tell us who the 'god' of whom he speaks was, perhaps the sun-god, or the god of vegetation . . . the oxen may have been incarnations of the god of vegetation". I believe the god of the mistletoe and the oak to have been that Hu of whom I have already spoken. Now we will recall that the image of "Darvel Gadarn" which was burned at Smithfield in 1538 had oxen offered up to it. I believe this image to have been the oak tree in an anthropomorphic or man-like shape. It appears to have been of wood, and, of course, we know that Darvel Gadarn was merely another name for Hu Gadarn, the god of Plenty, invariably associated in Keltic folklore with the ox, indeed in his symbolized form the ox itself.

It seems probable that the mistletoe as the symbol of the essence of life was introduced into the ritual of initiation of the Secret Tradition just as wheat was in that of the Eleusinian mysteries. We find it regarded as a cure for many kinds of disorders. It must indeed have been looked upon as the primordial agency of life itself. Were the "pearls" on the rim of the Cauldron of Inspiration mistletoe berries? This may appear very far-fetched, but I believe it to be not improbable. Did Hu or Arthur bring back from *Annwn* not only the Cauldron of Inspiration but the secret of life as emblemed by the mistletoe?

Much has been written regarding the human sacrifice of the Druids. To which god or gods was this sacrifice made? We are informed that huge images of wickerwork were erected, and that these were filled with victims, either criminals or slaves. The only trace of British gods designed in wickerwork which I can discover is that connected with the figures of Gog and Magog, the giants in the Guildhall. In a curious anonymous work entitled *The Giants in Guildhall*, published in 1741, and now exceedingly scarce, it is stated that the figures they replaced in 1708 were made of wickerwork. Let us look for a moment into the genealogy of Gog and Magog.

In wellnigh two thousand years of existence Imperial London has succeeded in retaining a wealth of folklore and legend quite commensurate with her importance and celebrity. It is significant, however, to the student of her tradition that at least eighty per cent. of it is Keltic and pre-Keltic, and of exceedingly venerable origin. Roman, Saxon, and Norman occupations have scarcely coloured London's pristine and native mythology, the associations of which are as Brythonic every whit as those of the folk-tales of Cambria.

Indeed, London's very name seems to be referable to certain British deities, her tutelary patrons. Doctor Henry Bradley, a sound authority, has explained "London" as a possessive formed from some such appellation as Londinos, derived from the old Keltic adjective meaning "fierce", and Mr. Gordon Home, the recent historian of Roman

London, gives it as his opinion that "the only conclusion at which it is possible to arrive is that the twin hills beside the Thames formed at some remote period the possession, and doubtless the stronghold, of a person or family bearing the name Londinos".

This is sound, and clear enough so far as it goes, but who were the "Fierce Ones" of the twin hills beside the Thames? If reference be made to the names of other British cities more or less coeval with London, it will at once be seen that a very considerable proportion of them received their names from tutelary or guardian deities. Camulodunum, or Colchester, is merely the dun or hill of Camulus, the Keltic war-god, the name of Eboracum, or York, has been traced to the Iberian divinity Ipor or Hyperion, and Corinium, or Cirencester, was the city of Corineus, an eponymous deity of the island. There are literally scores of examples. Thus it seems highly probable that London was named not after any tribe or gens, but from a sub-title of the gods who presided over the region.

Nor are there lacking the titles and traditions of gods whose characteristics well merit the formidable description preserved in the place-name. From time immemorial, almost, the names of Gog and Magog have been associated with the site. Its legendary appellation Cockaigne, as indigenous to it as Lyonesse to Cornwall or Alba to Scotland, has time and again been explained as "the land or region of Gog", the pleasant place or paradise of the Keltic Ogmios. Indeed, there is no dubiety concerning the veridically British character of the twin titan-deities Gog and Magog. Their figures were formerly carved into the slope of Plymouth Hoe, the **Gogmagog Hills in Cambridgeshire still embalm the** memory of their names, and the carved and painted statues of them which loom up at the farther end of the Guildhall are the successors of those once carried through the streets of the capital on Michaelmas Day, at the festival of the Lord Mayor's Show.

In his *New View of London* (1708), Hatton assures us that hackney coachmen in the City were wont to swear "by Gog and Magog", and he further makes it clear that a very vivid terror inspired certain Londoners, even at that late date, at the mere mention of them. Some apprentices, he tells us, were as "frighted at the names of Gog and Magog as little children are at the terrible sound of Raw-head and Bloody-bones", and evinced a livelier fear of them than at the prospect of being haled before the Lord Mayor or Chamberlain. Surely a terror so long-established could have survived only on account of an exceptionally powerful folk-memory of ancient sacrifices to the deities in question, and the student of tradition is probably justified in equating the giants of London with Ogmios, the fierce Keltic god of eloquence, who, garbed in lion-skin, and with club in hand, drew all men after him in chains and demanded more than occasional human holocausts. Magog, the "Mother Gog", is evidently his female counterpart, and her replacement by a male figure of Corineus is evidently a late and faltering acquiescence in the bowdlerized British mythology of Geoffrey of Monmouth and John Milton. Probably, too, the name Og, or Ogmios, became confused in later times, and by the same "authorities", with those of Gog and Magog, the Biblical monarchs of the Land of Bashan. On the whole, then, it appears highly probable that the twin hills on either side of the Walbrook were regarded as the duns or mounts of Og and his consort, just as the twin rocks at the extremity of Land's End were once regarded as their citadels.

There can be no doubt that Gog and Magog were deities of fertility, but it is also clear that Gog was one and the same with the Keltic Ogmios, the god of poetry and inspiration. Magog, it may be inferred, was also associated with the inspirational faculty. This would equate her with Keridwen, and indeed I see no reason to think that she is not one and the same with that goddess, who in more than one place is described as "the old giantess". But the important thing for us is that in the capital of England in pre-Roman times the rites of these monstrous deities were actually celebrated, and that the memory of them remained for so long. We are informed by more than one writer that the people of London in the eighteenth century almost worshipped them, and seemed in a sense to regard them as the palladia of the nation. Even now, were these effigies to be removed from their ancient positions in the Guildhall one can envisage something of the anger which would ensue.

Do we not take too much for granted that the passage of time utterly overwhelms ancient belief, and that during the past century we have made such strides in thought and progress as entirely to discount what we label the "superstitions" of other ages? True, there may have been during the past sixty or seventy years a much more wholesale breakaway from old tradition than ever before, but it is certain that only a very few generations ago British people were much more closely in touch with the remnants of the faith ancillary to the Secret Tradition than many moderns imagine. Festivals like Shrovetide and Yule are undoubtedly remnants of Druidic ritual, but it is equally clear that they enshrine many survivals from pre-Keltic practice. At Martinmas Saint Martin is said to have been cut up and eaten in the form of an ox. This is clear evidence that St. Martin merely took the place of the god Hu, who was symbolized by that animal. The Irish Tailteann Games still hold the memory of Tailtiu the fostermother of Lug, who died in the Kalends of August, and Lammas was the ancient Keltic feast of Lug himself. Another ancient British rite, in all probability associated with the Secret Tradition, survives in the annual celebration at Coventry of the Festival of Godiva. Who and what precisely was Godiva?

Godiva's historical existence is by no means at stake. Her personal reality is at once conceded. She was the mother not only of the patriotic Saxon princes Edwin and Morcar, but also of a heroine with associations even more romantic than her own, Edith Swan-neck, wife of that Harold who fell at Senlac or Hastings. But, this notwithstanding, the story of her noble sacrifice is demonstrably of the nature of legend. Roger of Wendover, who first alludes to it, wrote in the beginning of the thirteenth century, or about a hundred and fifty years after the death of the central figure. No previous chronicler makes mention of her unselfish performance, and in the eyes of the folkloreist it embraces so many circumstances obviously connected with ancient British religious rite as makes it evident that it must have arisen therefrom.

It is, indeed, quite unnecessary to prove, as has been done, that Coventry was, at the supposed date of the Countess's famous ride, a village inhabited by some three hundred serfs dwelling in wooden huts, that it had no market-place, nor groaned under the tolls and taxes alluded to in the legend. But it is of importance that Godgifu or Godiva, and her husband Leofric, Earl of Mercia, were the restorers, if not the founders, of its monastery of St. Osburg. For, with the restoration of this religious house, the prosperity of Coventry as a market-town commences. Godiva came to be regarded as a civic benefactress, consequently it is not surprising to find that her fame was confounded at a later date with the myth of the ancient British local goddess Brigantia or Brigit, whose story, during the early Christian centuries, had itself grown dim and confused in the popular imagination. In the Keltic period, this divinity, or her human representative, rode through the village of Coventry at the period of the summer festival at the end of May. But her feast and attributes were in the course of time confounded with and latterly absorbed by the legend of the fair-haired Saxon Countess.

This is a process with which the mythologist is well acquainted. The memory of a god wanes, and his legend is appropriated by a later hero or saint, with modifications of time and place. Just as in Ireland the goddess Brigantia, with whom we have here to deal, became the Christian St. Bridget, there is no reason to doubt that in Coventry a similar process took place, and that Brigantia or Brigiddu became confused with the saintly Godgifu, the "God-given".

For our contention, the salient points of Godiva's legend are that she passed through Coventry innocent of any covering save that of her abundant golden hair, and that in doing so, she was spied upon. There is good proof that the ancient Keltic deity, or a woman representing her, appeared in this condition at her annual festival ; and to spy upon godhead, or its representative, was, of course, the unpardonable sin, punished with the deprivation of sight.

That Coventry was anciently situated in a district in which Druidical rites were practised is generally conceded. At the village of Southam, hard by, the Godiva procession was formerly celebrated with a faithfulness equal to that evinced in the larger township. But curious variations of the ceremony, even more eloquent of its Druidical character than the rite obtaining at Coventry, were celebrated there. The pageant was headed by a personage known as "Old Brazen-Face", who wore a mask representing a bull's head, with horns complete. At certain festivals the hide and head of a sacrificed bull were worn by the Druidic officiants, so that "Old Brazen-Face" may well be regarded as the degenerate descendant of these. His name is, of course, an appellation of the Keltic sun-god, whose burning visage, surrounded by lambent rays, was frequently cast in brazen discs. The expression "Old" is frequently prefixed to the names of discredited deities, as in "Old Scratch", "Old Harry". Then came Godiva in a lace mantle, followed by a second Godiva, whose body was *stained black*. This, Pliny tells us, is precisely how the women of the ancient Britons decorated themselves on occasions of religious festival, smearing their bodies with woad, "so that they resembled the swarthy Ethiopians". At Fenny Compton, not far from Southam, where this Godiva rite is held, is Woad Farm, perhaps the very site where the plants from which the dye was made were formerly obtained. That a preponderatingly British element has survived in Warwickshire has been maintained by generations of archæologists, and what more probable than that it continued the practice of its ancient rites, placating later Christian opinion by their attribution to the saintly identity of a worthy daughter of Mother Church?

Coventry was formerly situated near the southern boundaries of the great British tribe of the Brigantes, the presiding deity of whom was the goddess Brigantia or Brigiddu, the same, as has been indicated, with the Irish Brigit, later Christianized into St. Bridget. She was also known as Danu or Anu, and is undoubtedly identical with that "Black Annis" who was supposed to lurk in the Dane (or Danu) Hills in Leicestershire, and to carry off children and sheep to her cavern—a memorial of human and animal sacrificial offerings. She was a divinity of the earth, a goddess of fertility, worshipped almost exclusively by women. The name "Black Annis" obviously relates to her woad-stained appearance, and accounts for the "Black Godiva". But how to explain "Peeping Tom"? The shrine of Brigiddu at Kildare, in Ireland, was enclosed by a fence which no man might pass *or peep through*, nor was any man permitted to gaze upon the sacred virgins dedicated to the goddess. Thus, when one or more of them rode through the streets of British Coventry at the time of the festival of the goddess, no "Peeping Tom" dared offend, or the outraged deity would summarily have deprived him of sight. To such a custom, then, we may trace the beginnings of the Godiva legend.

There can be little doubt that this rite has a certain bearing on the ritual of the Secret Tradition. Not only does it show its capacity for survival, but I think it reveals part of the representation gone through in the initiatory ceremony, or at least that it is associated with the ritual of the faith ancillary to the Tradition itself. Briginda was a goddess of knowledge, she was worshipped by poets, and had two sisters of the same name connected with leech-craft and smithwork. She was indeed a goddess of culture and poetry, and is the equivalent of the Gaulish goddess Brigindo. The name seems to come from the Welsh root "bri", "honour" or "renown". Her cult until lately was known in the Hebrides, where, on St. Bride's Day, Candlemas Eve, women dressed a sheaf of oats in female clothes, and set it with a club in a basket called "Bride's Bed", to the accompaniment of the cry : "Bride is come ! Bride is welcome !" She was undoubtedly, as Canon MacCulloch says, "an early teacher of civilization, inspirer of the artistic, poetic, and mechanical faculties, as well as a goddess of fire and fertility".

It seems to me that, like Keridwen, she presided over the female department of the ancient mysteries, as Hu presided over the male portion. In all likelihood her worship obtained more in the north and central parts of what is now England and Scotland, and in Ireland. But the fact that she is associated with wells, with inspiration, and with agriculture seems to equate her almost entirely with Keridwen, the goddess of the Sacred Cauldron.

CPSIA information can be obtained
at www.ICGtesting.com
Printed in the USA
LVHW061517041021
699479LV00025B/1454

9 781162 889016